Also by Thomas Kinsella

Poems and Translations *(1961)*
Nightwalker and Other Poems *(1968)*
The Táin *(1970)*

NOTES FROM THE LAND OF THE DEAD

AND OTHER POEMS

NOTES FROM THE

LAND OF THE DEAD

AND OTHER POEMS

THOMAS KINSELLA

ALFRED A. KNOPF • NEW YORK • 1973

Library of Congress Cataloging in Publication Data

Kinsella, Thomas.   Notes from the land of the dead.

I. Title.
PR6021.I35N66   1973   821'.9'14   73–7275
ISBN 0–394–48782–6
ISBN 0–394–70985–3 (pbk.)

"Drowsing over the Arabian Nights" originally appeared in *Four Quarters,*
November 1970. "The Clearing" and "Crab Orchard Sanctuary: Late Oc-
tober" originally appeared in *Antaeus,* Winter 1973.

Manufactured in the United States of America
First Edition

ACKNOWLEDGEMENTS

Grateful acknowledgement is made to the John Simon Guggenheim Memorial Foundation for a Fellowship spent in Ireland in 1968–69, when many of these poems were written or begun, and to the Cuala Press Limited, Dublin, for permission to reprint the contents of *Notes from the Land of the Dead*.

"Tear" was published in a limited edition by the Pym-Randall Press, Cambridge, Massachusetts, and in *Atlantis,* Dublin; "Nuchal (a fragment)" was issued with the 1970 patrons' portfolio of the Graphic Studio, Dublin; drafts of "Hen Woman" and "The High Road" were printed in *The Irish Press;* "Worker in Mirror, at his Bench" was printed in *The Malahat Review;* "Drowsing over the Arabian Nights" in *Four Quarters,* Philadelphia, Pennsylvania, and in *Soundings '72,* Blackstaff Press, Belfast; and a draft of "The Dispossessed" in *Threshold,* Belfast. Acknowledgement is made to the editors of these publications.

CONTENTS

Peppercanister Poems

NOTES FROM THE LAND OF THE DEAD

A snake out of the void moves in my mouth, sucks
at triple darkness. A few ancient faces
detach and begin to circle. Deeper still,
delicate distinct tissue begins to form,

hesitate, cease to exist, glitter again,
dither in and out of a mother liquid
on the turn, welling up from God knows what hole.

Dear God, if I had known how far and deep,
how long and cruel, I think my being
would have blanched: appalled.
                                    How artless,
how loveless I was then! O dear, dear God,
the times I had in my disarray—cooped up
with the junk of centuries! The excitement,
underlining and underlining in that narrow room!
—dust (all that remained of something) settling
in the air over my pleasures.
                                    Many a time
I have risen from my gnawed books
and prowled about, wrapped in a long grey robe,
and rubbed my forehead; reached for my instruments
—canister and kettle, the long-handled spoon,
metal vessels and delph; settled the flame,
blue and yellow; and, in abstracted hunger,
my book propped before me, eaten forkfuls
of scrambled egg and buttered fresh bread
and taken hot tea until the sweat stood out
at the roots of my hair!
                                    Then, getting quietly ready
to go down quietly out of my mind,
I have lain down on the soiled divan
alert as though for a journey
and turned to things not right nor reasonable.
At such a time I wouldn't thank
the Devil himself to knock at my door.

●

The key, though I hardly knew it,
    already in my fist.
Falling. Mind darkening.
    Toward a ring of mouths.
Flushed.
       Time, distance,
      meaning nothing.
            No matter.

•

I don't know how long I may have fallen
in terror of the uprushing floor
in my shell of solitude
when I became aware of certain rods of iron
laid down side by side, as if by giants,
in what had seemed the solid rock.
With what joy did I not hope, suddenly,
I might pass through unshattered
—to whatever pit! But I fell foul at the last
and broke in a distress of gilt and silver,
scattered in a million droplets of
fright and loneliness . . .
            So sunless.
That sour coolness . . . So far from the world and earth . . .
No bliss, no pain; dullness after pain.
A cistern-hiss . . . A thick tunnel stench
rose to meet me. Frightful. Dark nutrient waves.
And I knew no more.
          When I came to,
the air I drifted in trembled around me
to a vast distance with sighs
—not from any great grief, but disturbed
by countless forms drifting as I did,

wavery albumen bodies
each burdened with an eye. Poor spirits!
How tentative and slack our search
along the dun shore whose perpetual hiss
breaks softly, and breaks again,
on endless broken shells! Stare as we will
with our red protein eyes, how few we discover
that are whole—a shell here and there
among so many—to slip into and grow blank!
Once more all faded.
                              I was alone,
nearing the heart of the pit,
the light growing fitfully more bright.
A pale fume beat steadily through the gloom.
I saw, presently, it was a cauldron:
ceaselessly over its lip a vapour of forms
curdled, glittered and vanished. Soon I made out
a ring of mountainous beings, staring upward
with open mouths—naked ancient women.
Nothingness silted under their thighs
and over their limp talons. I confess
my heart, as I stole through to my enterprise,
hammered in fear.
                              And then I raised my eyes
to that seemingly unattainable grill
through which I must return, carrying my prize.

•

How it was done—that that pot should now
be boiling before you . . . I remember only snatches.
It must have been with utmost delicacy.
I was a mere plaything.

5

But perhaps
you won't believe a word of this.
Yet by the five wounds of Christ
I struggled toward, by the five digits
of this raised hand, by this key
they hold now, glowing, and reach out with
to touch . . . you shall have . . .

—what shall we not begin
to have, on the
count of

an egg of being

HEN WOMAN

The noon heat in the yard
smelled of stillness and coming thunder.
A hen scratched and picked at the shore.
It stopped, its body crouched and puffed out.
The brooding silence seemed to say "Hush . . ."

The cottage door opened,
a black hole
in a whitewashed wall so bright
the eyes narrowed.
Inside, a clock murmured "Gong . . ."

(I had felt all this before . . .)

She hurried out in her slippers
muttering, her face dark with anger,
and gathered the hen up jerking
languidly. Her hand fumbled.
Too late. Too late.

It fixed me with its pebble eyes
(seeing what mad blur?).
A white egg showed in the sphincter;
mouth and beak opened together;
and time stood still.

Nothing moved: bird or woman,
fumbled or fumbling—locked there
(as I must have been) gaping.

•

There was a tiny movement at my feet,
tiny and mechanical; I looked down.
A beetle like a bronze leaf
was inching across the cement,
clasping with small tarsi
a ball of dung bigger than its body.
The serrated brow pressed the ground humbly,
lifted in a short stare, bowed again;
the dung-ball advanced minutely,
losing a few fragments,
specks of staleness and freshness.

•

A mutter of thunder far off
—time not quite stopped.
I saw the egg had moved a fraction:
a tender blank brain
under torsion, a clean new world.

As I watched, the mystery completed.
The black zero of the orifice
closed to a point
and the white zero of the egg hung free,
flecked with greenish brown oils.

It slowly turned and fell.
Dreamlike, fussed by her splayed fingers,
it floated outward, moon-white,
leaving no trace in the air,
and began its drop to the shore.

•

I feed upon it still, as you see;
there is no end to that which,
not understood, may yet be noted
and hoarded in the imagination,
in the yolk of one's being, so to speak,
there to undergo its (quite animal) growth,
dividing blindly,
twitching, packed with will,
searching in its own tissue
for the structure
in which it may wake.
Something that had—clenched
in its cave—not been
now was: an egg of being.
Through what seemed a whole year it fell
—as it still falls, for me,
solid and light, the red gold beating
in its silvery womb,
alive as the yolk and white
of my eye; as it will continue
to fall, probably, until I die,
through the vast indifferent spaces
with which I am empty.

•

It smashed against the grating
and slipped down quickly out of sight.
It was over in a comical flash.
The soft mucous shell clung a little longer,
then drained down.

She stood staring, in blank anger.
Then her eyes came to life, and she laughed
and let the bird flap away.
"It's all the one.
There's plenty more where that came from!"

Hen to pan!
It was a simple world.

A HAND OF SOLO

Lips and tongue
wrestle the delicious
   life out of you.

A last drop.
Wonderful.
   A moment's rest.

In the firelight glow
the flickering
   shadows softly

come and go up on the shelf:
red heart and black spade
   hid in the kitchen dark.

Woman throat song
help my head
   back to you sweet.

●

Hushed, buried green baize.
Slide and stop. Black spades. Tray. Still.
Red deuce. Two hearts. Blood-clean. Still.

Black flash. Jack Rat grins.
She drops down. Silent. Face disk blank. Queen.

The Boss spat in the kitchen fire.
His head shook.

Angus's fat hand brushed in all the pennies.
His waistcoat pressed the table.

Uncle Matty slithered the cards together
and knocked them. Their edges melted. Soft gold.

Angus picked up a bright penny and put it
in my hand: satiny, dream-new disk of light . . .

"Go on out in the shop and get yourself something."
"Now, Angus . . ."
                          "Now, now, Jack. He's my luck."
"Tell your grandmother we're waiting for her."

She was settling the lamp.
Two yellow tongues rose and brightened.
The shop brightened.

Her eyes glittered.
A tin ghost beamed, Mick McQuaid
nailed across the fireplace.

"Shut the kitchen door, child of grace.
Come here to me.
Come here to your old grandmother."

Strings of jet beads wreathed her neck
and hissed on the black taffeta
and crept on my hair.

". . . You'd think I had three heads!"
My eyes were squeezed shut against the key
in the pocket of her apron. Her stale abyss . . .

Old knuckles pressed on the counter,
then were snatched away. She sat down at the till
on her high stool, chewing nothing.

The box of Indian apples
was over in the corner
by the can of oil.

I picked out one of the fruit,
a rose-red hard wax
turning toward gold, light like wood,

and went at it with little bites,
peeling off bits of skin
and tasting the first traces of the blood.

When it was half peeled,
with the glassy pulp exposed like cells,
I sank my teeth in it

loosening the packed mass of dryish beads
from their indigo darkness.
I drove my tongue among them

and took a mouthful, and slowly
bolted them. My throat filled
with a rank, Arab bloodstain.

THE HIGH ROAD

Don't be too long now, the next time.
She hugged me tight in behind the counter.
Here! she whispered. (A silvery
little mandoline, out of the sweet-box.)

They were standing waiting in the sun outside
at the shop door, with the go car,
their long shadows along the path.

A horse trotted past us down Bow Lane;
Padno Carty sat in the trap
sideways, fat, drifting along
with a varnish twinkle of spokes and redgold
balls of manure scattering
on the road behind.
                  Mrs. Fullerton
was sitting on a stool in her doorway,
beak-nosed, one eye dead.
DARK! DAAARK! squawked the sour parrot
in her room. (Sticking to his cage
with slow nails, upside down.
He mumbles on a bar, and creeps
stiffly, crossways, with his tongue;
a black moveable nut
                mumble
il my moulh.)
            Silvery tiny strings
trembled in my brain.
                  Over the parapet of
the bridge at the end of Granny and Granda's
the brown water poured and gurgled

over the stones and tin cans in the Camac,
down by the back of Aunty Josie's.
A stony darkness, after the bridge,
trickled down Cromwell's Quarters, step
by step, along by the foot of the wall,
from James's Street.

                (A mob of shadows
mill in silence on the Forty Steps;
horse-ghosts back and plunge, turning
under slow swords. In the Malt Stores,
through a barred window on one of the steps,
spectres huddle everywhere
among the shadowy brick pillars
and dunes of grain, watching
the pitch drain out of their wounds.)

Up the High Road I held hands,
inside on the path, beside the warm
feathery grass, and looked through the paling,
pulled downward by a queer feeling.
Down there . . . Small front gardens
getting lower and lower; doorways,
windows, below the road.
On the clay slope on the other side
a path slants up and disappears
into the Robbers' Den. I crept up
the last stretch to the big hole
full of fright, once, and knelt
on the clay to look inside:
it was only a hollow someone made,
with a dusty piece of man's dung
and a few papers in a corner,
and bluebottles.

                    (Not even in my mind
has one silvery string picked
a single sound. And it will never.)

Above the far-off back yards
the breeze gave a sigh: a sin happening . . .
I let go and stopped, and looked down
at a space in the weeds, and let it fall
for ever into empty space
toward a stone shed, and saw it turn
over with a tiny flash,
silvery shivering with loss.

ANCESTOR

I was going up to say something,
and stopped. Her profile against the curtains
was old, and dark like a hunting bird's.

It was the way she perched on the high stool,
staring into herself, with one fist
gripping the side of the barrier around her desk
—or her head held by something, from inside.
And not caring for anything around her
or anyone there by the shelves.
I caught a faint smell, musky and queer.

I may have made some sound—she stopped rocking
and pressed her fist in her lap; then she stood up
and shut down the lid of the desk, and turned the key.
She shoved a small bottle under her aprons
and came toward me, darkening the passageway.

Ancestor . . .   among sweet- and fruit-boxes.
Her black heart . . .
                              Was that a sigh?
—brushing by me in the shadows,
with her heaped aprons, through the red hangings
to the scullery, and down to the back room.

TEAR

I was sent in to see her.
A fringe of jet drops
chattered at my ear
as I went in through the hangings.

I was swallowed in chambery dusk.
My heart shrank
at the smell of disused
organs and sour kidney.

The black aprons I used to
bury my face in
were folded at the foot of the bed
in the last watery light from the window

(Go in and say goodbye to her)
and I was carried off
to unfathomable depths.
I turned to look at her.

She stared at the ceiling
and puffed her cheek, distracted,
propped high in the bed
resting for the next attack.

The covers were gathered close
up to her mouth,
that the lines of ill-temper still
marked. Her grey hair

was loosened out like
a young woman's all over
the pillow, mixed with the shadows
criss-crossing her forehead

and at her mouth and eyes,
like a web of strands tying down her head
and tangling down toward the shadow
eating away the floor at my feet.

I couldn't stir at first, nor wished to,
for fear she might turn and tempt me
(my own father's mother)
with open mouth

—with some fierce wheedling whisper—
to hide myself one last time
against her, and bury my
self in her drying mud.

Was I to kiss her? As soon
kiss the damp that crept
in the flowered walls
of this pit.

Yet I had to kiss.
I knelt by the bulk of the death bed
and sank my face in the chill
and smell of her black aprons.

Snuff and musk, the folds against my eyelids,
carried me into a derelict place
smelling of ash: unseen walls and roofs
rustled like breathing.

I found myself disturbing
dead ashes for any trace
of warmth, when far off
in the vaults a single drop

splashed. And I found
what I was looking for
—not heat nor fire,
not any comfort,

but her voice, soft, talking to someone
about my father: "God help him, he cried
big tears over there by the machine
for the poor little thing." Bright

drops on the wooden lid for
my infant sister. My own
wail of child-animal grief
was soon done, with any early guess

at sad dullness and tedious pain
and lives bitter with hard bondage.
How I tasted it now—
her heart beating in my mouth!

She drew an uncertain breath
and pushed at the clothes
and shuddered tiredly.
I broke free

and left the room
promising myself
when she was really dead
I would really kiss.

My grandfather half looked up
from the fireplace as I came out,
and shrugged and turned back
with a deaf stare to the heat.

I fidgeted beside him for a minute
and went out to the shop.
It was still bright there
and I felt better able to breathe.

Old age can digest
anything: the commotion
at Heaven's gate—the struggle
in store for you all your life.

How long and hard it is
before you get to Heaven,
unless like little Agnes
you vanish with early tears.

IRWIN STREET

Morning sunlight—a patch of clear memory—
warmed the path and
the crumbling brick wall,
and stirred the weeds sprouting
in the mortar.
                    A sparrow cowered
on a doorstep. Under the broken door
the paw of a cat reached out.
White nails fastened in the feathers.

Aware—a distinct dream—
as though slowly making it happen.
The suitcase in my hand.
                    My schoolbooks . . .

I turned the corner into the avenue
between the high wire fence and the trees
in the Hospital: under the leaves
the road was empty and fragrant
with little lances of light.
He was coming toward me—how
could he be there, at this hour?—
my maker, in a white jacket,
and with my face. Our steps
hesitated in awkward greeting.

                    •

Wakening again, upstairs,
to the same wooden sourness . . .

I sat up on the edge of the bed,
my hand in my pyjama trousers,
my bare feet on the bare boards.

a single drop

NUCHAL
(a fragment)

". . . down among the roots like a half-
buried vase brimming
over with pure water,
a film of clear brilliancy
spilling down its sides
rippling with reflections
of the four corners of the garden.
Fish-spirits slip down shimmering
into the grass; the grass
welcomes them with a hiss
of movement and voices
—its own snake-spirits.

On the last of the grass,
dreaming on one outstretched arm,
the woman lies smiling in her sleep.
Her arm dips over the brink
with the fingers trailing ladylike
in the water
              —the rivulet
simply wanders up to her,
making to go past out of the garden,
meets her fingers
—and four sunlit ripples
lengthen out from them;
the stream divides and subdivides
into four, moistening and softening
the first downward curve of the hill.

She has dreamed so long already
—it is monstrous . . .

四   four great rivers
creep across the plain
toward the four corners of
                    that vast domain:

Eastward, a quiet river feeds the soil
till the soft banks crumble, caked with oil.
A sudden shine, out of eternal spring:
a crop of gold, with many a precious thing
—bdellium, seeking the pearl in its own breast,
the flower-figured onyx, the amethyst . . .

Southward (it seems of melted gold) a stream
rolls toward the summer in a fiery gleam,
leaving a honey of fertility
to sweeten the salt marsh in some degree.

A third runs Westward in its deeper bed,
tigrish, through narrow gorges, winy red,
as though some heart toward which it ran (a vein)
drew it onward through that cruel terrain.

Lastly, a milk-white river, faring forth
in a slow flood, laughing to the North.

Four rivers reaching toward th'encircling sea,
that bitter river,
                    where every . . ."

ENDYMION

At first there was nothing. Then a closed space.
Such light as there was showed him sleeping.
I stole nearer and bent down; the light grew brighter,
and I saw it came from the interplay of our two beings.
It blazed in silence as I kissed his eyelids.
I straightened up and it faded, from his pallor
and the ruddy walls with their fleshy thickenings
—great raw wings, curled—a huge owlet-stare—
as a single drop echoed in the depths.

SURVIVOR

High near the heart of the mountain there is a cavern.
There, under pressure in the darkness,
as the walls protest and give dryly,
sometimes you can hear minute dust-falls.
But there is no danger.
The cavern is a perfect shell of force;
the torsions that brought this place forth
maintain it. It is spoken of, always,
in terms of mystery—our first home . . .
that there is a power holding this part of the mountain
subtly separate from the world, in firm hands;
that this cave escaped the Deluge;
that it will play some part on the Last Day.

Far back, a lost echoing
single drop:
the musk of glands
and bloody gates and alleys.

Claws sprang open
starred with pain.

•

Curled in self hate. Delicious.
    Head heavy. Arm too heavy,
What is it, to suffer:
    the dismal rock nourishes.
Draughts creep: shelter in them.
    Deep misery: it is a pleasure.
Soil the self.
    lie still.

Utter dread
    of moving
the lips
    to let out
the offence simmering
    weakly
as possible
    within.

Something crept in once.
Was that a dream?
A flame of cold that crept under the back
and under the head huddled close
into the knees and belly.
For what seemed a long year
a thin thread of some kind of sweetness
wailed far below
in the grey valley of the blood.
What is there to remember?

Long ago, abuse and terror . . .

O fair beginning . . .

landfall—an entire new world
floating on the ocean like a cloud
with a forest covering and clean empty shores.
We were coming from . . .   Distilled from the sunlight?
or the crests of foam?
                        From Paradise . . .
In the southern coast of the East . . . In terror
—we were all thieves. In search of a land without sin
that might go unpunished, and so prowling
the known world—the northern portion, toward the West

(thinking, places answering each other on earth
might answer in nature).
Late afternoon we came in sight
of promontories beautiful beyond description
and saw the crystal sea gather in savage currents
and dash itself against the cliffs.
By twilight everything was destroyed,
the only survivors a shoal of women
spilled onto the shingle, and one man
that soon—even as they lifted themselves up
and looked about them in the dusk—
they silently surrounded.
Paradise!
        No serpents.
No lions. No toads. No injurious rats
or dragons or scorpions. No noxious beasts.
Only the she-wolf . . .

Everyone falling sick, after a time.

Perpetual twilight . . . with most of the light dissolved
in the soil and rocks and the uneasy waves.
A last outpost into the gloom. Sometimes
an otherworldly music sounded in the wind.
A land of the dead.
        Above the landing place
the grass shivered in the thin shale
at the top of the path, waiting, never again disturbed.
There was a great rock in the sea, where we went down
—The Hag: squatting on the water,
her muzzle staring up at nothing.

A final struggle up rocks and heather,
heart and lungs aching,
and thin voices in the valley
faintly calling, and dissolving one
by one in the blood.

I must remember
and be able some time to explain.

●

There is nothing here for sustenance.
   Unbroken sleep were best.
Hair. Claws. Grey.
   Naked. Wretch. Wither.

AT THE CROSSROADS

A dog's
body zipped
open and
stiff in
the grass.

They used to leave hanged men here.

A night when the moon is full
and swims with evil through the trees,
if you walk from the silent stone bridge
to the first crossroads and stand there,
do you feel that sad disturbance under the branches?
Three times I have been halted there
and had to whisper "O Christ protect"
and not known whether my care was for myself
or some other hungry spirit.
Once by a great whiplash without sound.
Once by an unfelt shock at my ribs
as a phantom dagger stuck shuddering in nothing.
Once by a torch flare crackling
suddenly unseen in my face.
Three times, always at that same corner.
Never altogether the same. But the same.

Once when I had worked like a dull ox
in patience to the point of foolishness
I found myself rooted here, my thoughts
scattered by the lash Clarity:
the end of labour is in sacrifice,
the beast of burden in his shuddering prime
—or in leaner times any willing dogsbody.

A white face
stared from the
void, tilted over,
her mouth ready.

And all mouths everywhere so
in their need, turning on each furious
other. Flux of forms
in a great stomach: living meat torn off,
enduring in one mess of terror
every pang it sent through every thing
it ever, in shudders of pleasure, tore.

A white ghost flickered into being
and disappeared near the tree tops.
An owl in silent scrutiny
with blackness in her heart. She
who succeeds from afar . . .
                    The choice—
the drop with deadened wing-beats; some creature
torn and swallowed; her brain, afterward,
staring among the rafters in the dark
until hunger returns.

SACRIFICE

Crowded steps, a sea of white faces
streaked with toil.

The scrutiny is over, in sunlight,
terrible black and white.

There is the mark . . .   In those streaks . . .
Their hands are on her.
Her friends gather.
The multitudes sigh and bless
and persuade her heavily forward to her tears
in doomed excitement
down the cup of light
and onto her back on the washed bricks
with breasts held apart
and midriff fluttering in the sun.

The souls gather unseen, like wisps of hunger,
hovering above the table, not interfering,
as it is done in a shivering flash.
The vivid pale solid of the breast
dissolves in a crimson flood.
The heart flops in its sty.

•

Never mind the hurt. I've never felt
so terribly alive, so ready, so gripped
by love—gloved fingers slippery
next the heart!

Is it very difficult?

The blinding pain—when love goes direct
and wrenches at the heart-strings! But the pangs
quickly pass their maximum, and then
such a fount of tenderness!

                      Are you stuck?
Let me arch back.

                I love how you keep muttering
"You know now . . ."—and your concern . . .
but you must finish it.
I lose my mind gladly, thinking:
the heart—in another's clutches!

We are each other's knowledge. It is peace that counts,
and knowledge brings peace, even thrust crackling
into the skull and bursting with tongues of fire.
Peace. Love dying down, as love ascends.

I love your tender triumph, straightening up,
lifting your reddened sleeves. The stain spreads downward
through your great flushed pinions.
You are a real angel.
My heart is in your hands: mind it well.

nightnothing

ALL IS EMPTINESS,
AND I MUST SPIN

A vacancy in which apparently
I hang
     with severed senses

        •

I have been in places . . .

The floors crept,
an electric terror
waited everywhere
—just one touch!

We were made to separate
and strip. My urine flowed
with mild excitement.
Our hands touched lightly
in farewell.

Permit me, with drunken pleasure . . .

        •

How bring oneself to judge, or think,
so hurled onward!
        inward!

After a while, in the utter darkness,
there was a slight but perceptible
movement of the air.
It was not Death, but Night . . .

mountain coolness; a tiny
freshness of dew on the face
—tears of self forming.

I was lying in utter darkness
in a vaulted place. Cold air
crept over long-abandoned floors,
bearing a taint of remote iron
and dead ash: the interior
of some extinct . . .
                    A distant door
clangs. Echo of voices.

•

The sterile: it is a whole matter in itself.
Fantastic millions of
fragile

in every single

ELY PLACE

Sunday.
>   "Such a depth of charm
here always . . ."
>   Doomed in the sun.
In Mortuary Lane a gull
cried on one of the Hospital gutters
—I. I. I . . . harsh
in sadness, on and on,
beak and gullet open
against the blue.
>   Down at the corner
a flicker of sex, a white
dress, against the railings.

"This is where George Moore . . ."
>   rasps
his phantom walking-stick
without a sound, toward the Post Office
where her slight body, in white,
has disappeared.
>   (A flustered
perfumy dress—a mothering
shocked smile—live muscle
startling in skin.)

A blood vision
started out of the brick: the box
of keys in my pocket—I am opening it,
tongue-tied. I unpick the little
pen-knife and dig it in her throat,
her spirting gullet!
                    Vanishing . . .

Indoors, darkness pours down
through half light stale as the grave
over plates and silver bowls
glimmering on a side table.
Vanishing . . .
                    Solid matter
flickering in broad daylight

(and they are on it in a flash,
brief tongues of movement
ravenous, burrowing and feeding,
invisible in blind savagery,
upstreaming through the sunlight with it
until it disappears, buried
in heaven, faint, far off).

". . . with a wicked wit, but self-mocking;
and full of integrity behind it all . . ."

A few beginnings, a few
tentative tired endings over
and over . . .
                    Memoirs, maggots.
                              After lunch
a quarter of an hour at most
of empty understanding.

TOUCHING THE RIVER

That nude kneeling so sad-seeming
on her shelf of moss, how timelessly
—all sepia—her arm reaches down
to let her fingers, affectedly trailing,
stick in the stopped brown water.

Rivery movement; gurgling, clay-fresh;
light murmuring over the surface;
bubbling . . .
                Our unstopped
flesh and senses—how they vanish!

Though we kneel on the brink and drive our stare
down—*now*—into the current.
Though everywhere in the wet fields—listen—
the reeds are shivering (one clump of them
nestling a lark's eggs, I know, in a hoof-print).

THE LIFFEY HILL

The path climbs up to the left, toward the Plantation
(tree trunks, a clay floor, dim and still,
papers and bottles scattered everywhere
and lodging in the roots), then to the right
across the grass slope.
                              It opens onto the top,
a long field narrowing down
in bushes and wire at the far end

where the snow hushed
on Christmas morning
and we followed the rabbit tracks
dotted along light and powdery everywhere
and found the white silence
under a stillness of twigs
breathless with carefulness
where the rabbit went
                              where?
whirring past
                    a bird

Snow powdery pure
on the wool glove, detailed and soft.
The day lengthened, and the wool got dark and wet
and smelled of cold.
                              Flatsour? Raw . . . notsour

Morning, the magical-bright first print, gone . . .
The air grew dark, and harder.
We are out too late.
Voices, far away, die in the cold.

But there is still the pleasure of going home,
and dusk closing in, and a good fire.

I scrambled on top of the wall in the lamp-light,
bundled up in scarf and coat,
and hugged the iron post, and slipped down.
My boots scuffled on the path,
echoing, alone,
                    down the Lane.

GOOD NIGHT

It is so peaceful, at last:
the heat creeping through the house,
the floorboards reacting in the corner.
The voices in the next room
boom on in their cabinet.
How it brings out the least falseness!
There is one of them chuckling at
a quiet witticism of his own.

Relax, and these things
shall be . . .
        and the voices of a norm
that is in course of . . .
                foundering . . .
urgent yet mannerly:
I would remind . . . Please . . .
Oblivion, our natural condition . . .

and the sounds of the house are all
flowing into one another and turning
in one soft-booming, slowly swallowing
vertige most soothing and pleasant
down this suddenly live
brinegullet
         to a drowned pit
clasping the astonished spectre of
the psyche in its sweet wet.

Attached into the darkness by every sense
—the ear pounding—
peering eye-apples, unseeing—

fingers and tongue
                    outstretched—
into a nothingness
inhabited by a vague animal light
from the walls and floor.
Out of the glassy rock,
like tentacles moving on each other
near their soft roots, human thighs
are growing; if you look closely
you can see the tender undermost
muscle actually forming
from the rock, and the living veins
continuing inward, just visible
under the skin, and (faintly lit from within)
clusters of soft arms gathering down
tiny open eyes, finger-tips, pursed
mouths from the gloom, minute
drifting coruscations of light, glistening
little gnat-crescents of hair!

What essences, disturbed from what
profounder nothingness . . .
flickering, delicate
and distinct, fondled
blindly and drawn down
into what sense or languor

. . . Would you agree, then, we won't
find truths, or any certainties . . .

where monsters lift soft
self-conscious voices, and feed us
and feed in us, and coil
and uncoil in our substance,

so that in that they are there
we cannot know them, and that,
daylit, we are the monsters of our night,
and somewhere the monsters of our night are . . .
here . . . in daylight that our nightnothing
feeds in and feeds, wandering
out of the cavern, a low cry
echoing—Camacamacamac . . .

that we need as we don't need truth . . .

and ungulfs a Good Night, smiling.

OTHER POEMS

THE ROUTE OF THE TÁIN

Gene sat on a rock, dangling our map.
The others were gone over the next crest,
further astray. We ourselves, irritated,
were beginning to turn down toward the river
back to the car, the way we should have come.

We should have trusted our book —
after they tried a crossing, and this river too
"rose against them" and bore off
a hundred of their charioteers toward the sea
They had to move along the river Colptha
up to its source
         there:
where the main branch sharpens away gloomily
to a gash in the hill opposite;
then to Bélat Ailiúin
         by that pathway
climbing back and forth out of the valley
over to Ravensdale.

Scattering in irritation . . . who had set out
so cheerfully to celebrate our book;
cheerfully as we made and remade it
through a waste of hours, content to "enrich the present
honouring the past," each to his own just function . . .
Wandering off, ill-sorted,
like any beasts of the field,
One snout honking disconsolate,
another burrowing in its pleasures . . .

When not far above us a red fox
ran at full stretch out of the bracken
and panted across the hillside toward the next ridge.

Where he vanished—a faint savage sharpness
out of the earth—an inlet of the sea
shone in the distance at the mouth of the valley
beyond Omeath: grey waters crawled with light.

For a heartbeat, in alien certainty,
we exchanged looks. We should have known it, by now:
the process, the whole tedious
enabling ritual! Flux brought to fullness
—saturated—the clouding over—dissatisfaction
spreading slowly like an ache: something
reduced shivering suddenly into meaning
along new boundaries
                        —through a forest,
by a salt-dark shore,
by a standing stone on a dark plain,
by a ford running blood,
and along this gloomy pass, with someone ahead
calling and waving on the crest, against a heaven
of dismantling cloud—transfixed
by the same figure (stopped, pointing)
on the rampart at Cruachan
where it began . . .
the morning sunlight pouring on us all
as we scattered over the mounds
disputing over useless old books,
assembled in cheerful speculation
around a prone block, *Miosgán Medba*,
—Queen Medb's *turd* . . . ?—and rattled our maps,
joking together in growing illness
or age or fat; before us
the route of the Táin, over men's dust,
toward these hills that seemed to grow
darker as we drove nearer.

WORKER IN MIRROR,
AT HIS BENCH

I
Silent rapt surfaces
assemble glittering
among themselves.

A few more pieces.

What to call it . . .
                    Bright Assembly?
Foundations for a Tower?
Open Trap? Circular-Tending
Self-Reflecting Abstraction . . .

II
The shop doorbell rings.
A few people enter.

I'm sorry, I'm afraid you've caught me
a little early in my preparations.
Forgive me
                —the way they mess
with everything—
                    I am an indolent sinner.

Smile. How they tighten their lips:
What *is* it about the man
that is so impossible to like?
The flashy coat, the flourished cuffs?
The ease under questioning . . .

Yes, everything is deliberate.

This floppy flower. Smile.
This old cutaway style
—all the easier to bare the breast.
Comfortable smiles.
                    A cheap lapse—
forgive me: the temptation never sleeps.
The smiles more watery.

No, it has no practical application.
I am simply trying to understand something
—states of peace nursed out of wreckage.
The peace of fullness, not emptiness.

It is tedious, yes.
The process is elaborate, and wasteful
—a dangerous litter of lacerating pieces
collects. Let my rubbish stand witness . . .
Smile, stirring it idly with a shoe.
Take, for example, this work in hand:
out of its waste matter
it should emerge light and solid.
One idea, grown with the thing itself,
should drive it searching inward
with a sort of life, due to the mirror effect.
Often, the more I simplify,
the more a few simplicities go
burrowing into their own depths,
until the guardian structure is aroused . . .

Most satisfying, yes.
Another kind of vigour, I agree
—unhappy until its actions are more convulsed:
the "passionate"—might find it maddening.

Here the passion is in the putting together.

Yes, I suppose I am appalled
at the massiveness of others' work.
But not deterred; I have leaned my shed
against a solid wall. Understanding smiles.
I tinker with the things that dominate me
as they describe their random
persistent coherences . . .
clean surfaces shift
and glitter among themselves . . .

Pause. We all are vile . . .
Let the voice die away.

Awkward silence.
They make their way out.

But they are right to be suspicious
when answers distract and conceal.
What is there to understand?
Time punishes—and this
the flesh teaches. Emptiness,
is that not peace?

Conceal, and permit . . .
—pursuit at its most delicate,
truth as tinkering,
easing the particular of its litter,
bending attention on the remaining depths
as though questions had never been . . .

III

He bends closer, testing the work.
The bright assembly begins to turn in silence.
The answering brain glitters—one system
answering another. The senses enter
and reach out with a pulse of pleasure
to the four corners of their own wilderness:

a gold mask, vast
in the distance, stares back.
Familiar features.
Naked sky-blue eyes.
(It is morning
once upon a time.)
Disappears.
Was it a dream?
Forgotten.

Reappears: enormous
and wavering. Silver.
Stern and beautiful,
with something not yet pain in the eyes.
The forehead begins to wrinkle:
what ancient sweet time . . .
Forgotten.

Re-establishes:
a bronze head thrown back
across the firmament,
a bronze arm covering the eyes.
Pain established.
Eyes that have seen . . .
Forgotten.

Dark as iron.
All the light hammered
into two blazing eyes;
all the darkness
into one wolf-muzzle.
Resist!
An unholy tongue laps, tastes
brothers' thick blood.
Forget!

He straightens up, unseeing.

Did I dream another outline
in the silt of the sea floor?
Blunt stump of limb—
a marble carcase
where no living thing can have crept,
below the last darkness,
slowly, as the earth ages,
blurring with pressure.
The calm smile of a half-
buried face: eyeball
blank, the stare inward
to the four corners of
what foul continuum . . .

blackness—all matter
in one light-devouring
polished cliff-face
hurtling rigid
from zenith to pit
through dead

DROWSING OVER
THE ARABIAN NIGHTS

I nodded. The books agree,
one hopes for too much.
It is ridiculous.
We are elaborate beasts.

If we concur it is only
in our hunger—the soiled gullet . . .
and sleep's airy nothing;
and the moist matter of lust

(if the whole waste of women
could be gathered like one pit
under swarming Man . . .
—then all might act together!);

and the agonies of death,
as we enter our endless nights
quickly, one by one, fire
darting up to the roots of our hair.

THE CLEARING

". . . there is so little I can do any more
but it is nearly done . . ."

It is night. A troubled figure
is moving about its business
muttering between the fire and the gloom.
Impenetrable growth surrounds him
Owlful. Batful.
Great moths of prey.

". . . and still the brainworm will not sleep
squirming behind the eyes
staring out from its narrow box . . ."

He stops suddenly and straightens.
The eyes grow sharper
—and the teeth!

". . . and then the great ease
when something that was stalking us
is taken—the head cut off
held by the fur
the blood dropping hot
the eye-muscles star-bright to my jaws! . . ."

ST. PAUL'S ROCKS:
16 FEBRUARY 1832

A cluster of rocks far from the trade routes
a thousand miles from any other land
they appear abruptly in the ocean,
low-lying, so hidden in driving mists
they are seldom sighted, and then briefly,
white and glittering against the eternal grey.

Despite the lack of any vegetation
they have succeeded in establishing
symbiosis with the surrounding water.
Colonies of birds eat the abundant fish;
moths feed on the feathers; lice and beetles
live in the dung; countless spiders
prey on these scavengers; in the crevices
a race of crabs lives on the eggs and young.

In squalor and killing and parasitic things
life takes its first hold.
Later the noble accident: the seed, dropped
in some exhausted excrement, or bobbing
like a matted skull into an inlet.

THE DISPOSSESSED

The lake is deserted now
but the water is still clean and transparent,
the headlands covered with laurels,
the little estuaries full of shells,
with enchanting parterres where the waves
ebb and flow over masses of turf and flowers.

It was like a miracle, a long pastoral, long ago.
The intoxication of a life gliding away
in the face of heaven: Spring, a plain of flowers;
Autumn, with grape-clusters and chestnuts
formed in its depths; our warm nights
passing under starlight. We had established peace,
having learnt to practise virtue without
expectation of recompense—that we must be virtuous
without hope. (The Law is just; observe it,
maintain it, and it will bring contentment.)

Then, by the waterside, among the tortoises
with their mild and lively eyes, with crested larks
fluttering around Him, so light
they rested on a blade of grass
without bending it, He came among us
and lifted His unmangled hand:
                                These beauties,
these earth-flowers growing and blowing, what are they?
The spectacle of your humiliation!
If a man choose to enter the kingdom of peace
he shall not cease from struggle until he fail,
and having failed he will be astonished,
and having been astonished will rule,
and having ruled will rest.

Our dream curdled.
We awoke, and began to thirst
for the restoration of our house.
One morning, in a slow paroxysm of rage,
we found His corpse stretched on the threshold.

DEATH BED

Motionless—his sons—
we watched his brows draw together with strain.
The wind tore at the leather walls of our tent;
two grease lamps fluttered
at the head and foot of the bed.
Our shadows sprang here and there.

At that moment our sign might
have coursed across the heavens,
and we had spared no one to watch.

●

Our people are most vulnerable to loss
when we gather like this to one side,
around some death,

and try to weave it into our lives
—who can weave nothing but our ragged
routes across the desert.

And it is those among us
who most make the heavens their business
who go most deeply into this death-weaving.

As if the star might
spring from the dying mouth
or shoot from the agony of the eyes.

"We must not miss it,
however it comes."
—If it comes.

●

He stretched out his feet
and seemed to sink deeper in the bed,
and was still.
                    Sons no longer,
we pulled down his eyelids
and pushed the chin up gently to close his mouth,
and stood under the flapping roof.
Our shelter sheltered under the night.

                    ●

Hides, furs and skins,
are our shelter and our garments.

We can weave nothing.

CRAB ORCHARD SANCTUARY:
LATE OCTOBER

The lake water lifted a little and fell
doped and dreamy in the late heat.
The air at lung temperature—like the end of the world:
a butterfly panted with dull scarlet wings
on the mud by the reeds, the tracks
of small animals softening along the edge,
a child's foot-prints, out too far . . .

The car park was empty. Long threads of spider silk
blew out softly from the tips of the trees.
A big spider stopped on the warm gravel,
sunlight charging the dark shell.

A naked Indian stepped out onto the grass
silent and savage, faded,
grew transparent, disappeared.

A speedboat glistened slowly in the distance.
A column of smoke climbed from the opposite shore.
In the far inlets clouds of geese flew about
quarreling and settling in.

•

That morning
two thin quails appeared in our garden
stepping one by one with piping movements
across the grass, feeding. I watched a long time
until they rounded the corner of the house.
A few grey wasps still floated about at the eaves;
crickets still chirruped in the grass

—but in growing silence—after last week's frosts.
Now a few vacated bodies, locust wraiths,
light as dry scale, begin to drift
on the driveway among the leaves,
stiff little Fuseli devil bodies.
Hidden everywhere, a myriad
leather seed-cases lie in wait
nourishing curled worms of white fat
—ugly, in absolute certainty, piteous,
threatening in every rustling sound:
of bushes worrying in the night breeze,
of dry leaves detaching, and creeping.
They will swarm again, on suffocated nights,
with their endless hysterics; and wither away again.

•

Who will stand still then, listening
to that woodpecker knocking, and watch
the erratic jays and cardinals flashing
blue and red among the branches and trunks;
that bronze phantom pausing; and this . . .
                                        stock-still,
with glittering brain, withering away.

It is an ending already.
The road hot and empty, taken over
by spiders, and pairs of butterflies twirling
about one another, and grasshoppers leap-
drifting over the gravel, birds darting
fluttering through the heat.
                            What solitary step.

A slow hot glare out on the lake
spreading over the water.

WYNCOTE, PENNSYLVANIA: A GLOSS

A mocking-bird on a branch
outside the window, where I write,
gulps down a wet crimson berry,
shakes off a few bright drops
from his wing, and is gone
into a thundery sky.

Another storm coming.
Under that copper light
my papers seem luminous.
And over them I will take
ever more painstaking care.

PEPPERCANISTER
POEMS

The two poems that follow were published originally in Ireland by Pepper-canister, a small private publishing enterprise that Thomas Kinsella set up in 1972. Its purpose is to issue special items from time to time from Kinsella's home in Dublin, across the Grand Canal from St. Stephen's Church— known locally as "The Peppercanister."

Butcher's Dozen

13

Peppercanister *1, "Butcher's Dozen,"* was published in pamphlet form in April 1972, a week after the appearance of the Widgery Report. A tribunal had been set up by the British Government to inquire into the fatal shooting of thirteen civil rights demonstrators by the British Army in Derry on "Bloody Sunday," January 30th. The tribunal, under Britain's Lord Chief Justice Widgery, an ex-Army officer, startled those who had followed the evidence by virtually exculpating the Army.

The coffin device is derived from the badge issued for the Civil Rights Protest March in Newry on 6 February 1972.

The poem was read out in Derry during the public vigil on the first anniversary of the shootings.

BUTCHER'S DOZEN:

A LESSON FOR THE OCTAVE OF WIDGERY

I went with Anger at my heel
Through Bogside of the bitter zeal
—Jesus pity!—on a day
Of cold and drizzle and decay.
Three months had passed. Yet there remained
A murder smell that stung and stained.
On flats and alleys—over all—
It hung; on battered roof and wall,
On wreck and rubbish scattered thick,
On sullen steps and pitted brick.
And when I came where thirteen died
It shrivelled up my heart. I sighed
And looked about that brutal place
Of rage and terror and disgrace.
Then my moistened lips grew dry.
I had heard an answering sigh!
There in a ghostly pool of blood
A crumpled phantom hugged the mud:
"Once there lived a hooligan.
A pig came up, and away he ran.
Here lies one in blood and bones,
Who lost his life for throwing stones."
More voices rose. I turned and saw
Three corpses forming, red and raw,
From dirt and stone. Each upturned face
Stared unseeing from its place:
"Behind this barrier, blighters three,
We scrambled back and made to flee.
The guns cried *Stop*, and here lie we."
Then from left and right they came,
More mangled corpses, bleeding, lame,

Holding their wounds. They chose their ground,
Ghost by ghost, without a sound,
And one stepped forward, soiled and white:
"A bomber I. I travelled light
—Four pounds of nails and gelignite
About my person, hid so well
They seemed to vanish where I fell.
When the bullet stopped my breath
A doctor sought the cause of death.
He upped my shirt, undid my fly,
Twice he moved my limbs awry,
And noticed nothing. By and by
A soldier, with his sharper eye,
Saw the four elusive rockets
Stuffed in my coat and trouser pockets.
Yes, they must be strict with us,
Even in death so treacherous!"
He faded, and another said:
"We three met close when we were dead.
Into an armoured car they piled us
Where our mingled blood defiled us,
Certain, if not dead before,
To suffocate upon the floor.
Careful bullets in the back
Stopped our terrorist attack,
And so three dangerous lives are done
—Judged, condemned and shamed in one."
That spectre faded in his turn.
A harsher stirred, and spoke in scorn:
"The shame is theirs, in word and deed,
Who prate of Justice, practise greed,
And act in ignorant fury—then,
Officers and gentlemen,
Send to their Courts for the Most High

To tell us did we really die!
Does it need recourse to law
To tell ten thousand what they saw?
Law that lets them, caught red-handed,
Halt the game and leave it stranded,
Summon up a sworn inquiry
And dump their conscience in the diary.
During which hiatus, should
Their legal basis vanish, good,
The thing is rapidly arranged:
Where's the law that can't be changed?
The news is out. The troops were kind.
Impartial justice has to find
We'd be alive and well today
If we had let them have their way.
Yet England, even as you lie,
You give the facts that you deny.
Spread the lie with all your power
— All that's left; it's turning sour.
Friend and stranger, bride and brother,
Son and sister, father, mother,
All not blinded by your smoke,
Photographers who caught your stroke,
The priests that blessed our bodies, spoke
And wagged our blood in the world's face.
The truth will out, to your disgrace."
He flushed and faded. Pale and grim,
A joking spectre followed him:
"Take a bunch of stunted shoots,
A tangle of transplanted roots,
Ropes and rifles, feathered nests,
Some dried colonial interests,
A hard unnatural union grown
In a bed of blood and bone,

Tongue of serpent, gut of hog
Spiced with spleen of underdog.
Stir in, with oaths of loyalty,
Sectarian supremacy,
And heat, to make a proper botch,
In a bouillon of bitter Scotch.
Last, the choice ingredient: you.
Now, to crown your Irish stew,
Boil it over, make a mess.
A most imperial success!"
He capered weakly, racked with pain,
His dead hair plastered in the rain;
The group was silent once again.
It seemed the moment to explain
That sympathetic politicians
Say our violent traditions,
Backward looks and bitterness
Keep us in this dire distress.
We must forget, and look ahead,
Nurse the living, not the dead.
My words died out. A phantom said:
"Here lies one who breathed his last
Firmly reminded of the past.
A trooper did it, on one knee,
In tones of brute authority."
That harsher spirit, who before
Had flushed with anger, spoke once more:
"Simple lessons cut most deep.
This lesson in our hearts we keep:
Persuasion, protest, arguments,
The milder forms of violence,
Earn nothing but polite neglect.
England, the way to your respect
Is via murderous force, it seems;

You push us to your own extremes.
You condescend to hear us speak
Only when we slap your cheek.
And yet we lack the last technique:
We rap for order with a gun,
The issues simplify to one
—Then your Democracy insists
You mustn't talk with terrorists!
White and yellow, black and blue,
Have learnt their history from you:
Divide and ruin, muddle through,
Not principled, but politic.
—In strength, perfidious; weak, a trick
To make good men a trifle sick.
We speak in wounds. Behold this mess.
My curse upon your politesse."
Another ghost stood forth, and wet
Dead lips that had not spoken yet:
"My curse on the cunning and the bland,
On gentlemen who loot a land
They do not care to understand;
Who keep the natives on their paws
With ready lash and rotten laws;
Then if the beasts erupt in rage
Give them a slightly larger cage
And, in scorn and fear combined,
Turn them against their own kind.
The game runs out of room at last,
A people rises from its past,
The going gets unduly tough
And you have (surely . . . ?) had enough.
The time has come to yield your place
With condescending show of grace
—An Empire-builder handing on.

We reap the ruin when you've gone,
All your errors heaped behind you:
Promises that do not bind you,
Hopes in conflict, cramped commissions,
Faiths exploited, and traditions."
Bloody sputum filled his throat.
He stopped and coughed to clear it out,
And finished, with his eyes a-glow:
"You came, you saw, you conquered . . . So.
You gorged—and it was time to go.
Good riddance. We'd forget—released—
But for the rubbish of your feast,
The slops and scraps that fell to earth
And sprang to arms in dragon birth.
Sashed and bowler-hatted, glum
Apprentices of fife and drum,
High and dry, abandoned guards
Of dismal streets and empty yards,
Drilled at the codeword 'True Religion'
To strut and mutter like a pigeon
'Not An Inch—Up The Queen';
Who use their walls like a latrine
For scribbled magic—at their call,
Straight from the nearest music-hall,
Pope and Devil intertwine,
Two cardboard kings appear, and join
In one more battle by the Boyne!
Who could love them? God above . . ."
"Yet pity is akin to love,"
The thirteenth corpse beside him said,
Smiling in its bloody head,
"And though there's reason for alarm
In dourness and a lack of charm
Their cursed plight calls out for patience.

They, even they, with other nations
Have a place, if we can find it.
Love our changeling! Guard and mind it.
Doomed from birth, a cursed heir,
Theirs is the hardest lot to bear,
Yet not impossible, I swear,
If England would but clear the air
And brood at home on her disgrace
—Everything to its own place.
Face their walls of dole and fear
And be of reasonable cheer.
Good men every day inherit
Father's foulness with the spirit,
Purge the filth and do not stir it.
Let them out! At least let in
A breath or two of oxygen,
So they may settle down for good
And mix themselves in the common blood.
We all are what we are, and that
Is mongrel pure. What nation's not
Where any stranger hung his hat
And seized a lover where she sat?"
He ceased and faded. Zephyr blew
And all the others faded too.
I stood like a ghost. My fingers strayed
Along the fatal barricade.
The gentle rainfall drifting down
Over Colmcille's town
Could not refresh, only distil
In silent grief from hill to hill.

A Selected Life
In memory of Seán O Riada

Peppercanister 2, *"A Selected Life,"* *issued in July 1972, was written
in memory of Seán O Riada, Ireland's foremost composer, who died in
October 1971. O Riada's impact on the Irish consciousness, through his
documentary film music and his renewal of Irish traditional music, was
enormous, and his death was an occasion of national mourning.*

A SELECTED LIFE

I

GALLOPING GREEN: MAY 1962

He clutched the shallow drum
and crouched forward, thin
as a beast of prey. The shirt
stretched at his waist. He stared
to one side, toward the others,
and struck the skin cruelly
with his nails. Sharp
as the answering arid bark
his head quivered, counting.

II

COOLEA: 6 OCTOBER 1971

A fine drizzle blew
softly across the tattered valley
onto my glasses, and covered
my mourning suit with tiny drops.

A crow scuffled in the hedge
and floated out with a dark groan
into full view. It flapped up the field
and lit on a rock, and scraped its beak.
It croaked: a voice out of the rock
carrying across the slope. Foretell.

Foretell: the Sullane river winding downward
in darker green through the fields
and disappearing behind his house;

cars parking in the lane; a bare yard;
family and friends collecting in the kitchen;
a shelf there, concertinas sprawled in the dust,
the pipes folded on their bag.
The hole waiting in the next valley.
That.

       A rat lay on its side in the wet,
the grey skin washed clean and fleshy,
the little face wrinkled back in hatred,
the back torn open. A pale string
stretched on the gravel. Devil-martyr;
your sad, mad meat . . .

                 I have interrupted
some thing . . . You! Croaking
on your wet stone. Flesh picker.

The drizzle came thick and fast suddenly.
Down in the village the funeral bell began to beat.

•

And you. Waiting in the dark chapel.
Packed and ready. Upon your hour.
Leaving . . . A few essentials forgotten

—a standard array of dependent beings,
small, smaller, pale, paler, in black;

—sundry musical effects: a piercing
sweet consort of whistles crying,
goosenecked wail and yelp of pipes,
melodeons snoring in sadness,
drum bark, the stricken
harpsichord's soft crash;

—a lurid cabinet: fire's flames
plotting in the dark; hugger mugger
and murder; collapsing back in laughter.
Angry goblets of Ireland's tears,
stuffed with fire, touch. Salut!
Men's guts ignite and whiten in satisfaction;

—a workroom, askew; fumbling at the table
tittering, pools of idea forming.
A contralto fills the room
with Earth's autumnal angst; the pools coalesce.
Here and there in the shallows dim spirits
glide, poissons de la mélancolie.
The banks above are smothered in roses;
among their glowing harmonies, bathed in charm,
a cavalier retires in fancy dress,
embracing her loving prize; two baby angels,
each holding a tasseled curtain-corner,
flutter down, clucking and mocking complacently.
Liquids of romance, babbling
on the concrete floor. Let us draw a veil . . .

III
ST. GOBNAIT'S GRAVEYARD, BALLYVOURNEY:
THAT EVENING

The gate creaked in the dusk. The trampled grass,
soaked and still, was disentangling
among the standing stones
after the day's excess.

A flock of crows circled
the church tower, scattered
and dissolved chattering
into the trees. Fed.

His first buried night
drew on. Unshuddering.
And welcome . . .
Shudder for him,

Pierrot limping forward in the sun
out of Merrion Square, long ago,
in black overcoat and beret,
pale as death from his soiled bed,

swallowed back: animus
brewed in clay, uttered
in brief meat and brains, flattened
back under our flowers.

Gold and still he lay,
on his secondlast bed. *Dottore!* A withered smile,
the wry hands lifted. *A little while
and you may not . . .*

Salut.
Slán.
Yob tvoyu mat'.
Master, your health.

A Note about the Poet

Thomas Kinsella was born in Dublin in 1928. He worked in the Irish Department of Finance until 1965, when he came to the United States. He divides his time at present between Dublin and Philadelphia, where he is Professor of English at Temple University.

His first collection, Poems, was published in Ireland in 1956, followed by Another September in 1958, Downstream in 1962, Nightwalker and Other Poems in 1968, and, in 1969, The Táin, a translation of the eighth-century Irish prose epic Táin Bó Cuailnge, "The 'Cattleraid' of Cuailnge." This collection is his third to be published in the United States.

A Note on the Type

The text of this book was set in film in a type face called Griffo, a camera version of Bembo, the well-known monotype face. The original cutting of Bembo was made by Francesco Griffo of Bologna only a few years after Columbus discovered America. It was named for Pietro Bembo, the celebrated Renaissance writer and humanist scholar who was made a cardinal and served as secretary to Pope Leo X.

Sturdy, well balanced, and finely proportioned, Bembo is a face of rare ⋯ *n all of its sizes.*